CHAPTER II-19

THE SCIENCE OF COLOR

INVESTIGATING THE COLOR

THE SCIENCE OF COLOR

INVESTIGATING THE COLOR

Blue

Adapted from Donna Bailey's
Investigating Blue
by Barbara J. Behm

Gareth Stevens Publishing

MILWAUKEE

For a free color catalog describing Gareth Stevens's list of high-quality books, call 1-800-341-3569 (USA) or 1-800-461-9120 (Canada).

The editor would like to thank Anna Ciecka of the Department of Biological Sciences at the University of Wisconsin-Milwaukee for her assistance with the accuracy of the text.

Library of Congress Cataloging-in-Publication Data

Behm, Barbara J.
   Investigating the color blue / adapted from Donna Bailey's
Investigating blue by Barbara J. Behm. – North American ed.
     p. cm. -- (The science of color)
   Includes index.
   Summary: Investigates the color blue and where it appears in our
world, finding it in gems, in animals, and in people's eyes.
   ISBN 0-8368-1028-7
   1. Color--Juvenile literature. 2. Blue--Juvenile literature.
[1. Blue. 2. Color.] I. Bailey, Donna. Investigating blue.
II. Title. III. Series: Science of color (Milwaukee, Wis.)
QC495.5.B44 1993
535.6--dc20   93-23815

North American edition first published in 1993 by
Gareth Stevens Publishing
1555 North RiverCenter Drive, Suite 201
Milwaukee, WI 53212, USA

This U.S. edition is abridged from *Investigating Blue*, © 1993 by Zoë Books Limited, Winchester, England; original text by Donna Bailey, © 1993. Additional end matter © 1993 by Gareth Stevens, Inc.

Photographic Acknowledgements
The publishers would like to acknowledge, with thanks, the following photographic sources:

Cover, ZEFA Picture Library Ltd.; title, F. Jackson/Robert Harding Picture Library, p. 6, Trevor Hill; p. 7, Chris Fairclough Colour Library; pp. 9, 10, Trevor Hill; p. 13, NASA/Science Photo Library; p. 14, Robert Harding Picture Library; p. 15, Trevor Hill; p. 16 top, Jane Burton/Bruce Coleman Ltd.; p. 16 bottom, Robert Harding Picture Library; p. 17, Fritz Prenzel/Bruce Coleman Ltd.; pp. 18, 19, J. Allen Cash Photo Library; p. 20, Walter Rawlings/Robert Harding Picture Library; p. 21, F. Jackson/Robert Harding Picture Library; p. 22, Jane Burton/ Bruce Coleman Ltd.; p. 23 top and bottom, Trevor Hill; p. 24, J. Allen Cash Photo Library; p. 25, Chris Fairclough Colour Library; p. 26, Trevor Hill; p. 27 top and bottom, St. Bartholomew's Hospital, London/Science Photo Library

Printed in the United States of America

1 2 3 4 5 6 7 8 9 99 98 97 96 95 94 93

CONTENTS

Words that appear in the glossary are printed in **boldface** type the first time they occur in the text.

THE SCIENCE OF BLUE

When the Sun is shining, the sea and sky look blue. When the weather is cloudy, they lose their blueness. Without light from the Sun, we cannot see bright colors.

When you look at soap bubbles, you can see all the colors of the rainbow. White light can be split into the seven colors of the rainbow, or into what is known as the **spectrum**. The colors of the spectrum are red, orange, yellow, green, blue, indigo, and violet.

The spectrum

When you drop a pebble in the water, waves spread out from it. The distance between the top of one wave and the top of the next is called a **wavelength**. Light rays from the Sun travel to Earth in waves. Each color in the spectrum has a different wavelength. The wavelengths vary from short to long.

The invisible spectrum

We cannot see all of the rays in the entire spectrum. But even though we cannot see some of these rays, we can still feel them.

Those beyond the red end of the spectrum we feel as heat. Beyond the violet end of the spectrum are **ultraviolet rays**, **X rays**, and **gamma rays**.

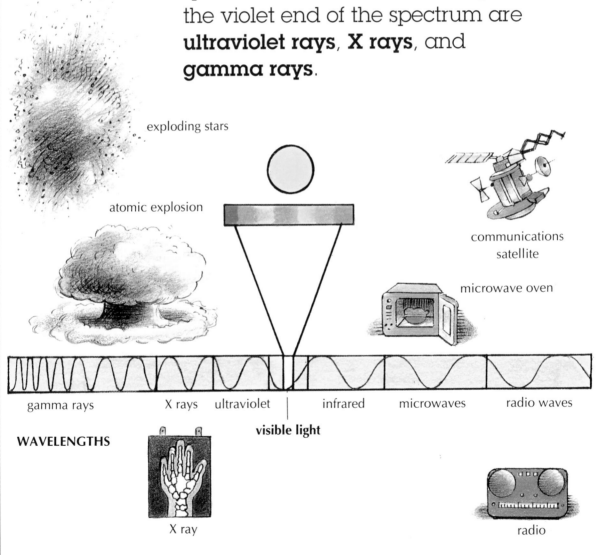

exploding stars

atomic explosion

communications satellite

microwave oven

| gamma rays | X rays | ultraviolet | infrared | microwaves | radio waves |

visible light

WAVELENGTHS

X ray

radio

Ultraviolet light

Ultraviolet rays can pass a short distance into the cells of living things. In animals, these cells use energy from ultraviolet rays to produce vitamin D for strong bones and teeth. Ultraviolet light can also be used to destroy germs in food. But too many ultraviolet rays can burn living plants and animals and may lead to skin cancer.

Mixing light

Red, green, and blue are called the **primary colors** of light. Mixing pairs of these primary colors together results in what are known as **secondary colors**. Mixing blue and red makes magenta; mixing blue and green makes cyan; mixing red and green makes yellow. Mixing all three primary colors together makes white.

primary colors of light

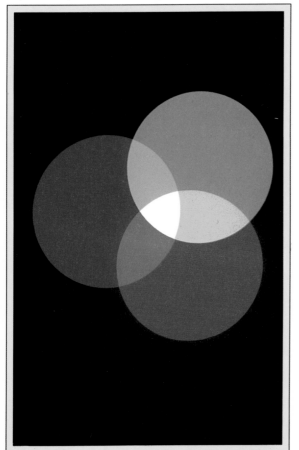

secondary colors of light

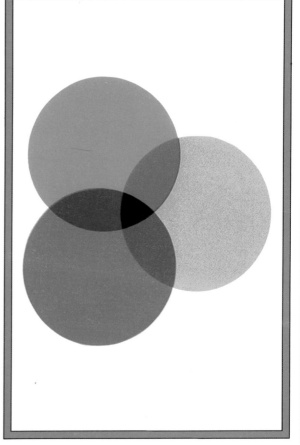

Mixing paint

Mixing paint is different from mixing light. Paints contain **pigments** that reflect the light of their own color and absorb light from other colors. The primary colors of paint are red, blue, and yellow. Mixing equal amounts of red and blue makes the color mauve; red and yellow make orange; blue and yellow make green. Mixing all the primary colors equally makes black.

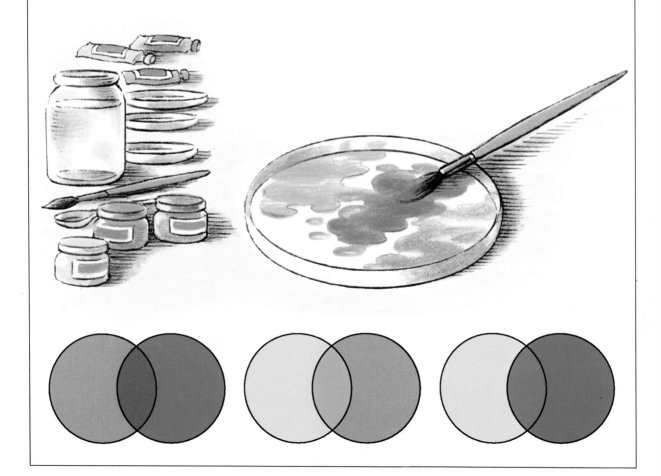

Color television

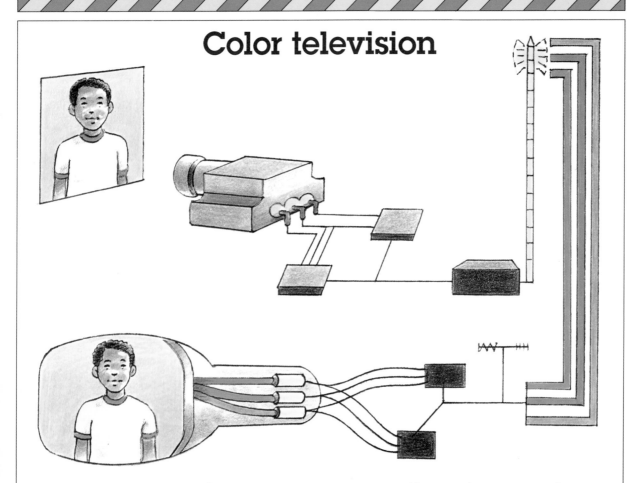

Color television uses the primary colors of light. A television camera splits the colors of an image into red, green, and blue. The colors enter tubes that send out a signal for each color. The signals are sent to TV sets, where they enter a device called a **scanner**. The scanner reads the signals to create a picture. One signal codes for red light. The second codes for green light. The third codes for blue light. If red, green, and blue are all blended together, white light results.

BLUE IN THE NATURAL WORLD

The sky looks blue during the day, but black at night. As the Earth spins on its **axis**, the Sun lights up the half of the Earth that is nearest the Sun. The other side of the Earth is in blackness because it gets no light from the Sun.

A "global" activity:

Shine a flashlight on a globe. Notice how much of the globe you can light with just one flashlight. Since light can travel only in straight lines, it cannot light the entire globe at once.

Blue sky

When light from the Sun travels to the Earth, it passes through gases and dust in the atmosphere. As the rays of light pass through these tiny particles, the blue light is scattered more than the other colors in the spectrum because of its short wavelength. This is what makes the sky look blue. Mountains will often reflect, or return, rays into the atmosphere. Blue light from both the Sun and the mountains is scattered more widely than the other colors, and the mountains look blue.

Blue flames

The flame on a gas ring of a stove looks blue. The blue flame is caused by burning natural gas, which is made of the gases hydrogen and methane.

In the center of the flame is a dark blue area that is actually cold, unburned gas and air.

Blue pigments

Long ago, artists had to make their own paints from natural materials. The ancient Egyptians made a bright blue paint by grinding a **mineral** called azurite.

Cobalt is a metallic element that was used by Chinese potters in ancient times to decorate china and porcelain. Patterns from this time have since become popular throughout the world.

Blue dyes

For thousands of years, people have
used plants to obtain a blue dye. The
plant in the picture above is called
indigo. Indigo was first used in India
and Egypt to dye cloth blue.

Certain berries, such as elderberries,
can create a blue-black dye. The
juice of blackberries is used as a deep
purple-blue dye.

Do this activity only if you have permission from an adult.

To tie-dye a t-shirt:

1. In several areas on a t-shirt, take some of the material and twist it.
2. Tie off the twists with rubber bands.
3. Put the shirt in some blue dye and allow enough time for it to soak in.
4. Carefully remove the t-shirt from the dye and remove the rubber bands from the t-shirt.
5. Rinse the t-shirt and hang it to dry.

Blue gems

Some of the gemstones found in rocks and soil are blue. Sapphires are among the world's most precious gems. They come in various shades of blue. Turquoise is also blue. American Indians have made turquoise jewelry for many centuries. These necklaces were made by members of the Navajo tribe.

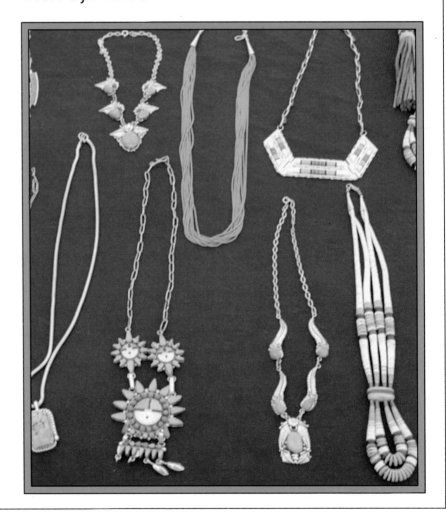

Blue feathers

The peacock, a male bird, has a bright blue head and neck and a blue-green body. The colors are made by the action of light on the feathers. Light passes through the outer cells, where red and yellow light is absorbed. Blue light is reflected to give an **iridescent**, or rainbow, effect. This effect changes depending on the angle from which you see it.

The blue of blue jays, kingfishers, and some parrots is caused by blue light reflected by the feathers. Other birds have a blue pigment in their feathers.

Butterflies and fish

Parrot fish live in coral reefs. Their bright colors help them compete for living space in the crowded seas. A butterfly's wings are covered with tiny scales that overlap each other. The scales reflect light, which then makes the different colors and patterns on its wings.

Blue flowers

The flowers of many plants have patterns of blue, yellow, and ultraviolet rays that attract insects. Near the center of a flower is a darker pattern called the nectar guide. This pattern shows an insect where to find the nectar on which it feeds.

Fungus

Fungus is a plant that decays **organic** materials. Often, fungus is blue-gray in color, like the fungus called **mold** found on bread. Some cheeses have veins of blue mold running through them. Fungus can cause disease in plants and animals, but it can also be very useful. Yeast is a fungus that makes bread rise. The mold that grows on bread and jam is used to make the medicine called **penicillin**.

> **Do not eat moldy food because it will make you sick. Wash your hands after touching the food and jars in the activity below.**

To grow mold:

1. Put pieces of bread, jam, apples, and cheese into separate jars.
2. Cover some of the jars.
3. Put some of the covered jars in the refrigerator, and put some on a sunny windowsill. Put the jars without covers outside.
4. Make a note of which food is the first to grow mold, and which is the last to grow mold. What are the best conditions for growing mold?

HUMANS AND BLUE

Blue has a calming effect on people. It is considered to be a "cool" color when compared to such "warm" colors as red and orange. Blue is a popular color for work clothes. In the United States, France, and China, many working people wear blue uniforms.

Blue eyes

People **inherit** the color of their eyes
from their parents. The father's **genes**
and the mother's genes together make
the eye color of their child. If both
parents have blue eyes, the child will
have blue eyes. If one of the parents
has brown eyes and one has blue
eyes, the child may have brown *or*

blue eyes. If both parents have brown eyes, the child may have either blue or brown eyes. Each parent has two eye-color genes – either two blue, two brown, or one of each. Brown-eye genes are **dominant**. This means if a parent has one brown gene and one blue gene, he or she will have brown eyes. Brown-eye genes are stronger than blue-eye genes, which are **recessive**. A parent with one brown-eye gene and one blue-eye gene can

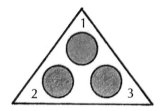 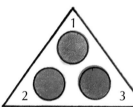 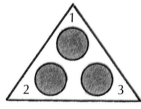 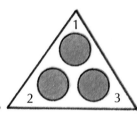

pass on a blue-eye gene to a child. If the other parent does the same, the child will have blue eyes.

An eye-color activity:

Ask several friends to draw a triangle with three circles inside it. Have them fill in the color of their mom's and dad's eyes in circles one and two. Have them fill in the color of their own eyes in circle three. Compare the results.

Veins and bruises

If you look at your wrists, you will see some blue **veins** just under the skin. The blood in your veins is not really blue. It just has less oxygen in it than the blood in your **arteries**. Blood that is rich in oxygen is bright red. The boy in the picture has bruised his eye. His skin appears blue because the blood vessels under the skin are damaged.

Blood and circulation

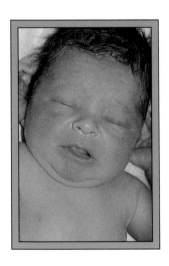

If it is very cold outside, the tips of your fingers may turn blue. Cold makes the blood vessels carrying blood to your fingertips get smaller so the blood cannot circulate to your fingers very well. Some babies are called "blue babies" because not enough oxygen is in their blood.

GLOSSARY

arteries: Vessels that carry blood away from the heart.

axis: The imaginary line that a turning object spins around.

dominant: Describes something that is stronger than something else.

gamma rays: Rays emitted by a radioactive substance.

genes: A tiny part of an animal or plant that determines a feature that will be passed on to the offspring.

inherit: To be given something from parents or other relatives from past generations.

iridescent: Colored like a rainbow.

mineral: A natural substance that has not been formed from plants or animals. Salt, rocks, and metals are all minerals.

mold: A kind of fungus that forms a fuzzy, blue-gray coating on the surfaces of damp or decaying substances.

organic: Matter that is or has been living and growing.

penicillin: Any of the antibiotic drugs made from mold. The drugs are used to treat diseases and infections.

pigment: The coloring matter in inks and paints. Natural pigments are found in plants and animals.

primary colors: The colors that cannot be made up from any other colors.

recessive: Describes something that is pushed back or held in reserve.

scanner: A device that senses or reads data.

secondary colors: The colors made when two primary colors are mixed together.

spectrum: The range of different wavelengths that includes the colors of light.

ultraviolet rays: Certain waves that are beyond the visible spectrum at the violet end.

veins: Vessels that carry blood to the heart.

wavelength: The distance between the top of one wave and the top of the next.

X rays: Powerful light rays that can pass through substances that ordinary rays of light cannot.

MORE BOOKS TO READ

Colors. Philip Yenawine (Delacorte)

The Invisible World of the Infrared. Jack R. White (Dodd, Mead, & Company)

Light and Color. Clarence Rainwater (Golden)

Looking at Light and Color. Julie Hill and Julian Hill (Batsford)

Over the Rainbow. The Science of Color and Light. Barbara Taylor (Random House)

The Rays of Light. (Greystone)

Simple Science Projects with Color and Light. John Williams (Gareth Stevens)

PLACES TO WRITE

Canadian Society for Color in Art, Industry, and Science
Institute for National Measurement Standards
NRC Ottawa, Ontario
K1A 0R6

Color Association of the United States
409 West 44th Street
New York, NY 10036

INDEX